Should We Pay for

WATER?

By Robert M. Hamilton

Published in 2018 by
KidHaven Publishing, an Imprint of Greenhaven Publishing, LLC
353 3rd Avenue
Suite 255
New York, NY 10010

Designer: Seth Hughes
Editor: Katie Kawa

Photo credits: Cover © istockphoto.com/fstop123; p. 5 (top) Andrew Mayovskyy/Shutterstock.com; p. 5 (bottom) Elena Elisseeva/Shutterstock.com; p. 7 (top-left) © istockphoto.com/Tim Hall; p. 7 (top-right) © istockphoto.com/le_cyclope; p. 7 (bottom-left) KSwinicki/Shutterstock.com; p. 7 (bottom-right) © istockphoto.com/Oli_Trolly; p. 9 Riccardo Mayer/Shutterstock.com; p. 10 BaLL LunLa/Shutterstock.com; p. 11 © istockphoto.com/AbeSnap23; p. 13 (left) thomas koch/Shutterstock.com; p. 13 (right) Kruit/Shutterstock.com; p. 15 antikainen/Thinkstock; p. 17 (top and bottom) Linda Parton/Shutterstock.com; p. 19 Neale Cousland/Shutterstock.com; p. 20 Sever180/Shutterstock.com; p. 21 (notepad) ESB Professional/Shutterstock.com; p. 21 (markers) Kucher Serhii/Shutterstock.com; p. 21 (photo frame) FARBAI/Thinkstock; p. 21 (inset, left) arindambanerjee/Shutterstock.com; p. 21 (inset, middle-left) Krisana Sennok/Shutterstock.com; p. 21 (inset, middle-right) Jimmy Tran/Shutterstock.com; p. 21 (inset, right) Juriah Mosin/Shutterstock.com.

Cataloging-in-Publication Data

Names: Hamilton, Robert M.
Title: Should we pay for water? / Robert M. Hamilton.
Description: New York : KidHaven Publishing, 2018. | Series: Points of view | Includes index.
Identifiers: ISBN 9781534523487 (pbk.) | 9781534523302 (library bound) | ISBN 9781534523296 (6 pack) | ISBN 9781534523319 (ebook)
Subjects: LCSH: Water-supply–Juvenile literature. | Water consumption–Juvenile literature. | Water-supply–Economic aspects.
Classification: LCC HD1691.H36 2018 | DDC –dc23

Printed in the United States of America

CPSIA compliance information: Batch #BS17KL: For further information contact Greenhaven Publishing LLC, New York, New York at 1-844-317-7404.

Please visit our website, www.greenhavenpublishing.com. For a free color catalog of all our high-quality books, call toll free 1-844-317-7404 or fax 1-844-317-7405.

CONTENTS

Paying for a
BASIC NEED

All living things need water to stay alive. Water is found in lakes, rivers, oceans, and the raindrops that fall from the sky. It's also found in homes and businesses—coming out of **faucets**, filling washing machines, and helping people get clean in showers and bathtubs.

Water is free in nature, but we pay for it to come into our homes and businesses. Some people believe all water should be free. Others believe there are important reasons we pay for water. Do you think we should pay for water? Read on to learn facts that will help you answer that question.

Know the Facts!

Water covers about 71 percent of Earth.

If water is free in nature and we need it to keep us alive, why should we pay for it? People have strong points of view on both sides of this **debate**.

A Useful UTILITY

Water is a natural resource. This means it's something found in nature that's useful for people. We drink water, and we clean our dishes, clothes, and bodies with water. We also use water in our toilets and our hoses, which water our plants and clean our cars.

Communities need water to fight fires, and farmers use water to grow the crops we need for food. Businesses use water, too, and water can be turned into electricity. We pay for the water we use for all these purposes. It's considered a utility, or a service provided to the public.

Know the Facts!

The average American uses as much as 100 gallons (378.5 l) of water each day.

We use water in many ways every day.

The Right to
WATER

Some people don't see why we should pay for the water we use. They believe people shouldn't have to pay for a basic human right. In fact, in 2010, the United Nations (UN), which is an **international** group that works to help people around the world, stated that all people should have the right to clean water. The UN also said clean water is necessary for all other human rights to be realized.

Does making people pay for water go against the idea that everyone should have access to this natural resource? Some people believe it does.

Know the Facts!

The UN stated that water should not cost more than 3 percent of a household's overall **income**.

People pay for water all over the world.

Storing Water
COSTS MONEY

Water may be a basic human right, but it costs money to get it to people. In most cases, people don't get their water from a well they dug on their land or from a nearby river or a lake. Water can come from water towers in communities, where it's stored until it's needed. Water is also held in reservoirs, or man-made lakes.

It costs money to build water towers and reservoirs. When we pay for water, we're paying in part for these storage **facilities**.

reservoir

Know the Facts!

The largest reservoir in the world is located in Africa.

A water tower is an important part of a community.

A Public Health
CONCERN

People who believe water should be free also note its importance to public health. Access to clean, safe drinking water is a public health concern. Public health is the overall health of entire populations. Water affects this in a major way.

Making people pay for water can harm those who don't have the money to afford it. This is certainly true in **developing** countries. Water is often more expensive in these nations than it is in countries such as the United States. Without access to affordable, clean water, the public health in these parts of the world suffers greatly.

Know the Facts!

As of 2010, people living in the poorest parts of Jakarta, Indonesia, pay more for water than people living in New York City.

If people can't afford water, their health suffers.

Clean and Safe
WATER

Access to clean and safe drinking water is necessary for the health of communities and nations. However, water isn't naturally clean and safe. It must be treated at a water treatment plant before being sent to homes and businesses.

At a water treatment plant, water is **filtered** to take out any **sediments** and tiny living things that might cause sicknesses. It's also treated with **chemicals** to make it safe to clean with and drink. The machines and chemicals needed to do this cost money, which comes from people paying their water bills.

Know the Facts!

The Safe Drinking Water Act was passed in 1974 and amended, or changed, in 1996. It set standards for the safety of drinking water in the United States.

When we pay for water, we're helping pay the cost of running water treatment plants that make water safe to drink.

Unsafe
WATER

If the water that comes into a person's home isn't clean, though, should they have to pay for it? This has become an important question after unsafe levels of lead were found in the water in Flint, Michigan, in 2015.

Lead is a metal that's found in nature, and it can end up in a community's water supply if the water isn't treated properly. Lead poisoning, or taking in too much lead, can cause health problems, often in children. Many people believe if the water coming into someone's home is unsafe, they shouldn't have to pay for it.

Know the Facts!

People who live in Flint pay more for water than many others in Michigan.

People **donated** bottled water to those living in Flint after lead was discovered in the water there. The events in Flint shed a light on the unfair practice of making people pay for unsafe water.

Money for WATER MAINS

In most cases, people are provided with clean, safe drinking water when they pay their water bills. The money they pay goes toward keeping the **process** of collecting and cleaning water running smoothly. It's also used to help get water to them.

Water reaches people's homes and businesses through a system of pumps and pipes. The pipes in this system are known as water mains. It costs money to keep these in good condition and to fix them if they break. Water main breaks can create big problems such as flooded streets.

Know the Facts!

Water that has been tested and is considered safe for drinking is called potable water.

Water has to travel a long way through pipes to get to some communities.

Considering
BOTH SIDES

Water takes a long journey to get to homes and businesses. People who think we should pay for water see the money as helping pay for the journey—the pipes, the storage facilities, and the treatments to make water clean and safe. However, there are some who believe no one should be charged for access to something they need to live, and certainly not if the water they're getting isn't safe.

After learning the facts, what do you think? Should we pay for water, or should water be free for everyone?

Know the Facts!

A water meter is used to measure the amount of water that comes to a home or business. This measurement is used to find out how much people should pay for water.

Should we PAY for WATER?

YES

- It costs money to build and keep up water storage facilities.

- Water must be treated to make sure it's safe and clean. This process costs money.

- When we pay for water, we're also paying for the pipes and pumps that take it to our homes and businesses.

NO

- Access to safe water was declared a basic human right by the UN, and people shouldn't have to pay for a basic right.

- People shouldn't have to pay for water that's not clean and safe.

- Making people, especially people living in poverty, pay for clean water is a public health concern.

Use this chart to help you remember both points of view on this important issue before deciding where you stand.

21

GLOSSARY

chemical: Matter that can be mixed with other matter to cause changes.

debate: An argument or discussion about an issue, generally between two sides.

developing: Having little money and a low standard of living compared with other countries.

donate: To give away freely.

facility: Something, such as a building, built for a specific purpose.

faucet: A device that controls the flow of water.

filter: To separate solid parts out of a liquid.

income: Money that comes from working.

international: Involving two or more countries.

process: A series of actions or changes.

sediment: Tiny bits of matter, such as sand, soil, or rock.

For More
INFORMATION

WEBSITES

EPA Water Sense Kids

www3.epa.gov/watersense/kids/index.html
The Environmental Protection Agency (EPA) created this website to teach young people about water usage through fun facts and a game.

"We Fear the Water"

www.theatlantic.com/photo/2016/02/we-fear-the-water/459687/
This collection of photographs from *The Atlantic* provides an up-close look at the water crisis in Flint, Michigan.

BOOKS

Bright, Michael. *From Raindrop to Tap*. New York, NY: Crabtree Publishing Company, 2016.

Olien, Rebecca. *Cleaning Water*. North Mankato, MN: Capstone Press, 2016.

Pipe, Jim. *Water*. King's Lynn, UK: BookLife, 2015.

INDEX